j974.7
Gun

D0876400

WITHDRAWN
MUSSER PUBLIC LIBRARY

GRAPHIC LIBRARY™

DISASTERS IN HISTORY

The TRIANGLE SHIRTWAIST FACTORY FIRE

by Jessica Gunderson

illustrated by Phil Miller
and Charles Barnett III

Consultant:
Clete Daniel, Professor of American Labor History
School of Industrial and Labor Relations
Cornell University, Ithaca, New York

Capstone
press

Mankato, Minnesota

Graphic Library is published by Capstone Press,
151 Good Counsel Drive, P.O. Box 669, Mankato, Minnesota 56002.
www.capstonepress.com

Copyright © 2006 by Capstone Press. All rights reserved.
No part of this publication may be reproduced in whole or in part, or stored in a
retrieval system, or transmitted in any form or by any means, electronic, mechanical,
photocopying, recording, or otherwise, without written permission of the publisher.
For information regarding permission, write to Capstone Press, 151 Good Counsel Drive,
P.O. Box 669, Dept. R, Mankato, Minnesota 56002.
Printed in the United States of America

1 2 3 4 5 6 11 10 09 08 07 06

Library of Congress Cataloging-in-Publication Data
Gunderson, Jessica Sarah, 1976–
    The Triangle Shirtwaist factory fire / by Jessica Gunderson ; illustrated by Phil Miller and
Charles Barnett III.
        p. cm.—(Graphic library. Disasters in history)
    Includes bibliographical references and index.
    ISBN-13: 978-0-7368-5483-2 (hardcover)
    ISBN-10: 0-7368-5483-5 (hardcover)
    1. Triangle Shirtwaist Company—Fire, 1911—Juvenile literature. 2. Clothing factories—
New York (State)—New York—Safety measures—History—20th century—Juvenile literature.
3. Labor laws and legislation—New York (State)—New York—History—20th century—Juvenile
literature. 4. New York (N.Y.)—History—1898–1951—Juvenile literature. I. Miller, Phil, ill. II.
Barnett, Charles, III, ill. III. Title. IV. Series.
F128.5.G95 2006
974.7'1041—dc22   2005029858

Art Direction and Design
Bob Lentz

Production Designer
Alison Thiele

Colorist
Buzz Setzer

Editor
Donald Lemke

Editor's note: Direct quotations from primary sources are indicated by a yellow background.

Direct quotations appear on the following pages:
Page 7, from Clara Lemlich's speech at Cooper Union, November 22, 1909, as quoted in
    Dave Von Drehle's *Triangle: The Fire that Changed America* (New York: Atlantic Monthly
    Press, 2003).
Page 8, from a speech on November 24, 1909, by Clara Lemlich, as quoted in Dave Von
    Drehle's *Triangle: The Fire that Changed America* (New York: Atlantic Monthly Press,
    2003).
Page 21, from an article originally published in the *Call,* November 23, 1909, as transcribed
    on Cornell University School of Industrial and Labor Relations' Kheel Center website
    (http://www.ilr.cornell.edu/trianglefire/texts/stein_ootss/ootss_sg.html).

TABLE OF CONTENTS

In November 1909, 400 Triangle Shirtwaist Factory workers and 15,000 other garment workers from New York City went on strike.

WE ARE STARVING WHILE WE WORK:
WE MIGHT AS WELL STARVE WHILE WE STRIKE!

While protesting their working conditions, many strikers were arrested.

Let us have a voice!

It's our right.

We know that if we stick together—and we are going to stick—we will win!

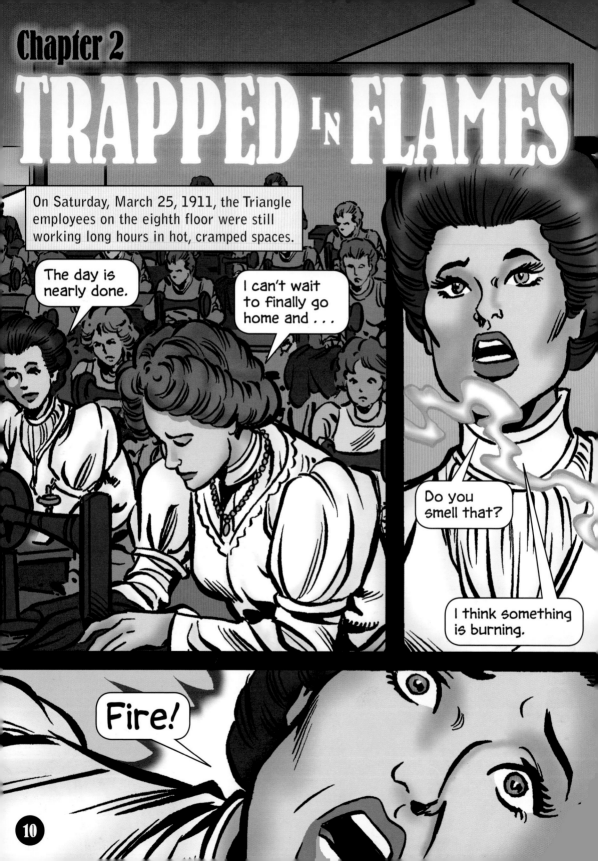

11

13

Harris and Blanck, the owners of the Triangle Factory, were charged with manslaughter because of the locked doors and unsafe fire escape.

They must suffer for killing our children!

Order in the court!

Eighteen days later, the trial was over . . .

Not guilty!

Though the men were acquitted on criminal charges, they were ordered to pay $75 to each victim's family.

Safer working conditions—now!

Ladies Waist & Dressmakers Union Local 25

We Mourn Our Loss

The Triangle fire made the public aware of the unsafe work environments of garment factories. Soon after, automatic sprinklers were installed in many buildings. Today, fire inspections and drills are enforced by law.

MORE ABOUT THE TRIANGLE FIRE

No one knows what caused the Triangle Shirtwaist Factory fire of 1911. Some people believe a match or lit cigar ignited a pile of rags on the eighth floor.

Although the exact number of deaths is unknown, 146 bodies were found after the fire. Twenty-three of the dead were men, but the rest were girls from ages 13 to 23. Seven bodies remained unidentified.

Most of the young women at the Triangle Factory were immigrants of Jewish or Italian heritage. Many lived on New York's East Side, many blocks from the factory.

In 1911, laws requiring fire drills didn't exist in New York. Most workers at the Triangle Factory had never practiced how to escape the building during a fire. Today, businesses need to have fire alarms and an emergency action plan. The plan must include safe exit routes for employees.

The Asch Building, which housed the Triangle Shirtwaist Factory, was nearly fireproof. The outside of the building suffered only minor damage, though everything inside the structure burned. Today, the building is a National Historic Landmark and part of the New York University campus.

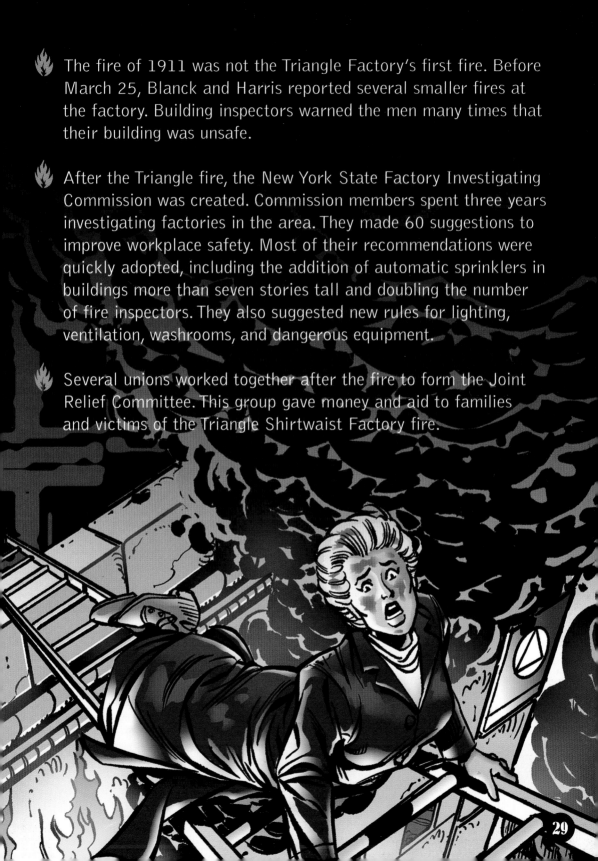

The fire of 1911 was not the Triangle Factory's first fire. Before March 25, Blanck and Harris reported several smaller fires at the factory. Building inspectors warned the men many times that their building was unsafe.

After the Triangle fire, the New York State Factory Investigating Commission was created. Commission members spent three years investigating factories in the area. They made 60 suggestions to improve workplace safety. Most of their recommendations were quickly adopted, including the addition of automatic sprinklers in buildings more than seven stories tall and doubling the number of fire inspectors. They also suggested new rules for lighting, ventilation, washrooms, and dangerous equipment.

Several unions worked together after the fire to form the Joint Relief Committee. This group gave money and aid to families and victims of the Triangle Shirtwaist Factory fire.

GLOSSARY

acquit (uh-KWIT)—to find someone not guilty of a crime

manslaughter (MAN-slaw-tur)—the crime of killing someone without intending to do so

mourner (MOR-nuhr)—a person who is very sad and grieving for someone who has died

strike (STRIKE)—refusing to work because of an argument or disagreement with an employer over wages or conditions of the workplace

union (YOON-yuhn)—an organized group of workers set up to help improve such things as working conditions, wages, and health benefits

INTERNET SITES

FactHound offers a safe, fun way to find Internet sites related to this book. All of the sites on FactHound have been researched by our staff.

Here's how:

1. *Visit www.facthound.com*
2. Type in this special code **0736854835** for age-appropriate sites. Or enter a search word related to this book for a more general search.
3. Click on the **Fetch It** button.

FactHound will fetch the best sites for you!

READ MORE

Crewe, Sabrina, and Adam R. Schaefer. *The Triangle Shirtwaist Factory Fire.* Events That Shaped America. Milwaukee: Gareth Stevens, 2004.

Landau, Elaine. *The Triangle Shirtwaist Factory Fire.* Cornerstones of Freedom. New York: Children's Press, 2005.

Woog, Adam. *A Sweatshop During the Industrial Revolution.* The Working Life Series. San Diego: Lucent Books, 2003.

BIBLIOGRAPHY

Greenwald, Richard A. *The Triangle Fire, the Protocols of Peace, and Industrial Democracy in Progressive Era New York.* Labor in Crisis. Philadelphia: Temple University Press, 2005.

The Kheel Center, Cornell University ILR School. *The Triangle Factory Fire.* http://www.ilr.cornell.edu/trianglefire

McClymer, John F. *The Triangle Strike and Fire.* American Stories. Fort Worth, Texas: Harcourt Brace College Publishers, 1998.

Stein, Leon. *The Triangle Fire.* Ithaca, N.Y.: Cornell University Press, 2001.

Von Drehle, Dave. *Triangle: The Fire that Changed America.* New York: Atlantic Monthly Press, 2003.

INDEX